THE

THINKER

❝ I thought about the new pornographic
lamb chop panties. I thought about
the <u>Queen</u> <u>Mary</u> standing on end alongside the Empire State Building and
how they'd ever get it back in the
water. I thought about the birds and
the bees and wondered what the hell
they had to do with sex. I thought
about sex (my best thought of the
morning thus far). I thought about a
chimpanzee in the Bronx Zoo who is
a latent Homo sapiens. Then I thought
about sex again, just to keep on my
toes. I thought about Errol Flynn's
autobiography and wondered how he
found the time. Then my friend
Beveridge Wernfuld arrived, leading a
full-grown saber-toothed tiger on a
dental-floss leash. The last thing
I remember is Beveridge saying,
'Sick 'im!' ❞

Never Trust a
Naked Bus Driver

was originally published
by E. P. Dutton & Co.,
Inc., at $2.50.

Also by the Author

NEVER TRUST A NAKED BUS DRIVER

JACK DOUGLAS

⚓ PERMABOOKS • NEW YORK

This Permabook includes every word contained in the original, higher-priced edition, plus new material written especially for this edition by the author. It is printed from brand-new plates made from completely reset, clear, easy-to-read type.

NEVER TRUST A NAKED BUS DRIVER

E. P. Dutton edition published April, 1960

PERMABOOK edition published May, 1961
1st printing.........................March, 1961

PERMABOOK editions are distributed in the U.S. by Affiliated
Publishers, Inc., 630 Fifth Avenue, New York 20, N.Y.

PERMABOOK editions are published in the United States by
Pocket Books, Inc., and in Canada by Pocket Books of Canada,
Ltd.—the world's largest publishers of low-priced adult books.

To
Barry and Ella Fitzgerald

But really and truly
to
Betty Bruce

Never Trust a Naked Bus Driver

CHAPTER

1

May This House Be Safe from Alexander King

ON THURSDAY, August 29, 1947, in the bull ring at the Spanish town of Linares, Manolete, the great matador, was killed by a bull. This and many other fascinating stories are not included in my new book, *Never Trust a Naked Bus Driver*.

The present title of the book is a substitution for the title I originally wanted to use. I *had* intended to call it: *How to Make a Million Dollars and Speak Correct English and Be Good Looking and Sexy and Healthy and Well Read and Perfectly Groomed and What*

Wines to Order with What Courses and Write Popular Music and Learn Taxidermy in Your Spare Time but just before we went to press, I found out there *is* a book with that title. Just my stinking luck, eh, Herbie?

Nevertheless, as a progressive midget once said, "Onward and Upward." My next book, of course, will be autobiographical. (It's getting to be about that time.) And let's face it, that's the best kind of book to write nowadays, especially if you're a reformed drunk, or a reformed opium smoker, or a reformed shoplifter. Of course I'll be working under a handicap, because I'm not a reformed *anything*. (It's still going on.)

Nevertheless, as a progressive German midget once said; *"Machen Sie sich keine Sorgen."*

* * *

When I was seven years old, for my birthday, my folks let me steal a bicycle of my very own. When I was eight years old, I stuck up a candy store. I *had* to. Although I had been discharged from Lexington as completely cured, suddenly every nerve in my body started screaming—I needed a jelly bean fix. Just my luck they'd run out of jelly beans, so I forced Old Man Krine to open the cigar box where he kept the money, and it wasn't a bad haul, $45,000, to be exact.

I hear you saying $45,000 is a lot of money for a neighborhood candy store—but little do you realize that the candy store was just a front—in the back they melted stolen Volkswagens. (And it didn't take long in a pressure cooker.)

However, back to our ordeal. Old Man Krine seemed to resent the fact that I was sticking him up, so he started to give me some spiel about he always thought I was such a wonderful boy, so neat and tidy, and manly, and kind and sweet, and so I shot him.

This abrupt change of pace seemed to unnerve him, and as he lay there in a pool of surprise, he had an extremely odd expression on his face, which I assume came from the fact that it probably was the first time in his candy store career that he'd ever been shot in the belly by a Boy Brownie. (I should say quickly, a *disbarred* Boy Brownie.) I had been drummed out of the troop the summer before, because I had refused to salute Havelock Ellis (who was our den mother).

* * *

Needless to say, because of my extreme youth I was not prosecuted for making Old Man Krine porous. And so with my forty-five thousand tucked safely away in my rompers, I left home in search of adventure. And in less than a week, I met the girl of my dreams. And she looked just the way I had pictured her in my dreams. Tall. Short. Thin. Fat. Blonde and brunette. We were married at the Radio City Music Hall. After the ceremony, she excused herself to go to the ladies' room and I never saw her again. But I read about it in the newspapers. It seems she'd taken a wrong turn somewhere and had been kicked to death by the Rockettes. From that day to this, I've never felt quite the same toward precision.

A Day at the Beach

or

Drip! Went the Strings of My Heart

SHE WAS BEAUTIFUL and she was young and she rose from the sea in the rosy dawn. She walked up the beach and into an abandoned shack and called a name:

"Sol! Ohhh Sol! It's me—it's Mabel! Sol???"

But no one answered. Because there was no one there to answer. Sol had drowned some seventy-eight years before. In the surf in front of the abandoned shack. He and Mabel had gone swimming together that day. Mabel had been swimming a long time. She lost all track of time when she swam. And now she was back. Calling.

"Sol! Ohhh Sol! It's me. It's Mabel!—Sol???"

CHAPTER
3

Dialogue

1st MAN
You wanna buy a legitimate dog?

2nd MAN
No—we got a dog.

1st MAN
Whatsamatter—couldn'tcha wait?

2nd MAN
Couldn't I wait for what?

1st MAN

Till you met *me*.

2nd MAN

How did I know you were trying to sell a dog?

1st MAN

You coulda guessed.

2nd MAN

Look, I'm a stranger in town—and I never saw you before in my life.

1st MAN

Here—you can have the dog for nothi... (*Hands him the dog.*)

2nd MAN

But—I toldja—we got a dog.

1st MAN

You got *two* dogs.

2nd MAN

Oh—yeah. I forgot.

1st MAN

You oughta do something about that memory of yours.

2nd MAN

You wanna buy a dog?

1st MAN

How much?

8

other Romans because of Article 865 Sec. 34 in the Folk Singers Union. Not taking baths added an aura of authenticity when one played and sang such folk tunes as: "Don't lift your leafy arms to pray, or we'll be burning incense all day," and "Hildegard—get out in the yard," and "Twenty-four hours in the galleys don't make you no bosom pallies," and "Don't fence me in."

Androcles got his inspiration for his self-composed folk songs by wandering in a small forest near his summer home. It was a very small forest, just three trees, two bushes, and an abandoned toupé (that had been tinted green by Howard Johnson).

Androcles loved to walk in the forest alone, because the peace and quiet of the leafy glades was very conducive to meditation and contemplation. He smiled to himself as he strolled the well worn path. He was thinking of Jeanie with the light brown hair and how he hated light brown hair. Why couldn't Jeanie have been a flaming redhead, or a breath-of-spring blonde, or even bald? Jeanie was the one who introduced Androcles to The-Lion-with-the-Thorn-in-His-Paw (he was a calypso singer and "The-Lion-with-the-Thorn-in-His-Paw" was his billing when he played at the Virgin Islands Inn) in the Virgin Islands (which are islands in the West Indies and named after Sol Virgin, the famous Israeli explorer). Androcles, true to tradition, pulled the thorn from the paw of the lion, which he never should have done, because The-

Lion-with-the-Thorn-in-His-Paw never worked again —as a calypso singer. He *did* get a few jobs as a lion, but just being a lion hardly paid the gas bill.

Rome, if you've read your history books, was a rather far-out city in those days, what with the orgies, the Saturnalias (orgies), and rose festivals (orgies), and also at the Colosseum they had really big shows like bulls fighting bears, men with nets fighting men with spears, full-scale naval battles, a few legion (Roman) drill teams, and a Miss Rheingold contest (Rheingold in those days was considered very daring), and last, but not least, the next to closing act was always the Martyrs versus the Lions. And of course, the opening of the season, Caesar himself always threw out the first martyr. And there was never a scarcity of martyrs then like there is now—there were martyr schools everywhere. Androcles had a diploma from one of these, the best one, the Martyr's Studio it was called where one learned to become a method martyr —actually the only worthwhile type of martyr.

Three years after Androcles had pulled the thorn from the Lion's paw they met again, under rather different circumstances, in the arena at the Colosseum. The lion was still a lion, but Androcles was no longer a folk singer—he was now a full-time martyr.

The Colosseum was brimming over with blood-thirsty Romans that sunny day in 69 B.C. but Androcles recognized the lion as the one from which he had withdrawn the thorn, and, of course, the lion recognized Androcles, and he smiled, and Androcles smiled back. They both stood there smiling at each other for a long full minute, then suddenly the lion snarled: "You son-of-a-bitch! You wrecked my career! So now, do you know what I'm going to do to you?"

"You're not going to do anything," replied Androcles, shooting the lion squarely between the eyes.

Moral: It is better to be a folk singer with a pure heart and a loaded pistol than a lion who uses profanity.

5

*Department of Better
Understanding*

"The Geisha Girl"

THE JAPANESE geisha girl has one mission in life—the
entertainment of men. Her role is unknown in Western
civilization and is widely misunderstood. Most of us
picture the geisha girl as a prostitute.

My Wife and I Were "Just Friends" Until I Started Taking Bernstein's Buffalo Bombs

(A story of love rekindled on upper Park Avenue)

LOOKING out of my window, this glorious fall morning, I knew immediately it was fall because all the penthouses were turning brown. After tomato juice, a vodka, and a Bloody Mary, I began to feel better until suddenly for no good reason I started to think about Toynbee Doob. I didn't *want* to think about Toynbee

Doob, because I hated his guts (the rest of him I didn't mind so much). I thought about a lot of things I really didn't want to think about this morning. Did you know that every *fourth* baby born into this world is *Chinese?* This comes as quite a surprise sometimes, especially if the parents are Yugoslavian. Also, every twenty-third birth is twins. This too, can come as quite a surprise, especially if the twins are Yugoslavian and the parents are Chinese (and not even married).

I thou_ _____ _____ing else I didn't want to think about this morning. I thought of the time that Ralf Doob (Toynbee's sister) put a pair of Keds into an Osterizer and got a quart and a half of sneaker juice.

Just then, the writer, Beveridge Wernfuld, came into the room. Beveridge Wernfuld was the only writer I know who *looked* like a writer. He was eight feet seven inches tall, and had six fingers on each hand, which was ideal for television where you had to turn it out fast.

Beveridge paused dramatically, and lighted a cigarette. Then he *lit* a cigarette. Just to prove he could do it *both* ways. Then he threw himself into an easy chair and puffed through his nose (he'd had a filter installed in each nostril). Then he lowered his sequined lids and stared at me with his suede eyes (Beveridge Wernfuld was a very *rich* writer.) But I still felt sorry for him. His wife, the former Bo-Bo Deshler-Wallich of Newport, Bar Harbor, Palm Beach, and the wet part of Oyster Bay, had been unfaithful to him with the corner newsboy (between sales).* Beveridge Wernfuld had *everything* except happiness. He had a fabulous estate in Beverly Hills, Bel Air, and the dry part of Santa Monica Bay.

At the "West Gate" of his fabulous estate two live elephants were chained, each holding an old-fashioned carriage lamp, and trained to step on solicitors. Winding up the driveway, lined with poplars and footmen, one came to the house itself. Five hundred and seventy-three rooms, done in the simple manner of a cottage. Sort of a Cape Cod Buckingham Palace (surrounded by an Esther Williams moat). In back of the main house were stables with stalls for a hundred and fifty-four pure-bred stallions and their friends (with Esther Williams drinking troughs). But none of this meant anything to Beveridge Wernfuld anymore, because Beveridge Wernfuld was stuck! And there's nothing as stuck as a stuck writer. Beveridge Wernfuld's specialty was TV Westerns, and the man at the agency had insisted he come up with something new and different, or he was through!

That's why I felt sorry for him. He had used up every Western plot that had ever existed. And some that didn't. In wild desperation, Beveridge had really gone far out. I remember one where the "new schoolmarm" turned out to be a Civil War draft dodger, which of course brought an awful lot of snotty mail from other Civil War draft dodgers. He had also writ-

---

* On windy days.

ten "Death Valley Days," "Death Valley Nights," "Death Valley Afternoons," "Breakfast in Death Valley," "People Are Funny in Death Valley," and "Who'll Haul Your Borax When I'm Gone, Baby?"

This, of course, shook the confidence of *everybody* at the agency to such a degree that one of the executives said: "Let's put *Wernfuld* on the train and see if he gets off at Westport."

I couldn't stand Beveridge's staring at me any longer, so I said, "Why don't you switch to *Private Eyes?*"

"You swine!" he screamed as he sprang up and slashed me on both cheeks with his saber.

As I stood there, bleeding to death, I thought to myself: "Beveridge Wernfuld is either insecure or a graduate of Old Heidelberg (or both)."

7

Songs My English Mother Thought She Could Sing

"When It's Tulip Time in Wessex, I'll Be Putting Gas in My Essex."

"When You're Punting on the Peconic, I'll Be Drinking Gin and Tonic."

"When It's Commander Whitehead Time in Nottingham, I'll Be Schweppsing Back To You."

"Who'll Screw In Your Monocle When I'm Far Away?"

"There'll Be Bluebirds Over The White Cliffs of Dover, So Watch It!"

8

The Most Unforgettable Marquis I Ever Met

LOOKING out of my window, this glorious fall morning, I knew immediately it was fall, because chorus boys all over town were losing their leaves. After a cup of black coffee, with a Roman candle in it (to really wake me), I started thinking about the most unforgettable Marquis I ever met.

* * *

One bright spring morning, the Marquis de Sade and I were sitting on the edge of the Grand Canyon (which is an off-Broadway hole) discussing girls, and the Marquis' viewpoint was, to say the least, *different.* I had always thought of girls as something to fondle and cuddle, make love to, and maybe marry, but the Marquis talked like he was doing research for a far-out cookbook (and he was). But, unfortunately, the Marquis lived in a chateau which forbade cooking in the rooms, so he'd had to buy a portable barbecue, and invite them out into the back yard, where suddenly the unsuspecting little darlings found themselves being basted by a bastard (as one of them so charmingly put it).

But the Marquis was a fascinating conversationalist. And under his protective armor of outward cruelty, he was a man of subtle fiendishness. With the Marquis de Sade the Little Bopeep story took on another meaning. The *sheep* weren't the ones who were in trouble. And in *his* version, Alice was *pushed* through the looking glass. He spoke of his lovely wife, whom he had met at an Elks picnic, where she had just won the three-legged race all by herself. (She was wearing high heels and a hip boot.) He had liked her immediately because she had dared to be different. (She was listed in the Yellow pages under Tripods.) He told me about their three lovely children, Debbie, Rodney, and Verve. Verve was the youngest and had come in a box of cornflakes (a very unusual prize, but the competition in the breakfast food game gets keener every day). The Marquis was very proud of Verve, because although he *could* have gone to Oxford or Cambridge, or even Princeton, he had become an international jewel thief instead. Which, of course, gave him a four-year head start on everybody from Oxford, Cambridge, and Princeton.

The more I got to know the Marquis de Sade the better I liked him. Which wasn't easy after some of the things I caught him doing. Like pulling the wings off Piper Cubs, helping old ladies across the East River, and giving that poor old man, who plays the violin on the sidewalk in front of Carnegie Hall, a poisoned dime.

I haven't seen the Marquis much recently. After he wired mother's bathtub (with mother in it) just to put some zip in his home movies, we sort of drifted apart.

9

Personal

AMAZE YOUR WIFE. Fly to Mexico today.

A Saber-Toothed Tiger May Be Out of Place in a French Provincial Living Room

LOOKING out of my window this glorious fall morning, I knew immediately it was fall, because when I stuck my head out of the window for a breath of fresh, some cull looked up at me from the sidewalk and yelled:

"Hey, ya son-of-a-bitch—it's fall!"

After a tall glass of Kirschwasser and a crust of black bread, I took my daily swim around Manhattan

Island. It seemed longer today, mainly I supposed because I had forgotten to take off my bathrobe.

I felt much better after a brisk rubdown with a velvet glove and a breakfast of live hummingbirds. (Very difficult to swallow, but they *do* keep you awake all day.)

My friend Beveridge Wernfuld was due at any moment, so I went into the bathroom to see if my hair was combed (over my eyes because I couldn't bear to look at him). Not that Beveridge was repulsive, but he was growing a mustache at the moment, and it was coming out green, with tiny yellow and pink blossoms here and there, and it was very distracting, when you were trying to *think*. And at that moment I was trying to think about *Of Human Bondage,* a book by Somerset Maugham. That book always worried me. It's about this guy with a clubfoot that gets kicked around by a broad. It always seemed to me that it should have been the other way around.

Beveridge Wernfuld still hadn't arrived, so I started thinking about other things. Like the Seven Wonders of the World: Mildred, Gladys, Mabel, Louise, Trixie, Babs, and Lily.*

I thought about the new pornographic lamb chop panties. The Wheaties Sports Federation. Mom's apple pie. The new thinking man's mousetrap (which allows the mouse a choice of hanging or shooting). I thought about the Queen Mary standing on end

---
* *My* world.

alongside the Empire State Building, and how they ever got it back in the water. I thought about the birds and the bees and wondered what the hell they had to do with sex. I thought about sex (my best thought of the morning so far). I thought of the Malthusian Theory of overpopulation and the mass starvation it would bring. I thought about Danny's Hideaway* slowly being turned into a garage, all because of Thomas Robert Malthus, and his lousy theory. I thought about Doctor Schweitzer's publicity man, and Harry Golden's homely philosophy about the U.S. mails. I thought about a chimpanzee in the Bronx Zoo who is a latent Homo sapiens (give up, Mr. Cerf?). I also thought about sending money to the Navajos so they can buy guns instead of sheep (let's hear it out there!). Then I thought about my second wife (whom I lost in a wishing well). Those things *really work,* don't they? Then I thought about sex again, just to keep on my toes. I thought about Errol Flynn's autobiography and wondered how he found the time. I thought about the satyr who was married to a nymphomaniac or to put it another way . . . the law of diminishing returns. Finally I was tired of thinking and it was just as well, because Beveridge Wernfuld arrived, leading a full-grown Saber-Toothed Tiger on a dental floss leash. The last thing I remember is when Beveridge said "Sic 'im!"

---

* New York restaurant owned by a cowboy movie star.

CAMP NOKOPOKOPOKONOMOPKO
BRIDGETON, MAINE

Julie 17, 1959

Dere Mom and Dead

Here I am at cammp again this year where you sent me again this year. This is the same camp you sent me to last year. And here I am again. At the same camp. Mr. Monhan who was the watter sking instructor up until very late last night. That is when they found his body. In a motel over in south Windham which is a little town near our camp which has a motel. mrs. Monhan who is mr. Monhan's wife did not cry at all because she was glad. That she shot him my coonseler told me. Thank you very much for the rain coat you sent me. I gave it to Herbie. I was wrong about what I said about my coonseler last year. He is not a fagg.

But I am.

Yore sunLouis

CHAPTER
12

Just Announced

The new magazine on the market called: *True Divorce*.

* * *

Cure for baldness. It isn't exactly a cure, but if you're bald, all you do is plant moss, and keep it damp. It's a little hard to part—but you'll never be troubled with dandruff, just toadstools.

* * *

An organization called Sports Cars, Anonymous. It's for guys who are trying to break the habit. Any time a member gets the urge to drive a sports car, he calls a fellow member, who comes over and sells him a motorcycle.

*   *   *

Discovery at Harvard. Some scientist has crossed a homing pigeon with a parrot, so that in case he gets lost he can ask questions.

13

A Song to Remember *

*"Just Before the Head-on Collision, Mother,
I Am Thinking, Dear, of You"*

JUST BEFORE the head-on collision, Mother, I am
thinking, dear, of you because—

You weren't like *other* mothers . . . you *wanted* me
to be a race car driver . . .

Right from the very beginning . . .

You bought me a crash helmet even before I had a
head.

I wanted a sister . . . or a brother . . . but *you* gave
me a *Corvette*.

---

* From the *Floyd Collins Songbook*.

I'll never forget my first big race . . . I was driving against the Champion . . .

Mickey Rooney. Poor Mickey . . . he shouldn't have done it. He drove his Volvo right in front of my Poo-Jo (pronounced "Peugeot") and I had to throw a lighted match into his gasoline tank. It may not have been the fair thing to do, but it sure was pretty.

After that, I just *had* to race, Mother. I just had to. Like Van Gogh had to cut off his ear . . . just because it was *there!*

I was getting better with every race, and pretty soon I hit the big time.

I finally got to be champion of the world, and then I met *her*. Petrovana Krine, the gorgeous ballet dancer. The way I met her was very unique. It was during a race. She danced out into the middle of the track. And she was beautiful, and what an idea—dancing "Swan Lake" in the middle of an automobile track, during a race. I could have *avoided* hitting her if I had *wanted* to, but I figured to myself: Would *I* drive my race car across the stage of the Metropolitan Opera House while *she* was doing her lousy dance? I think not.

But it was love on first impact, and we were married soon after that at Jones Beach, where we drank champagne out of each other's swim fins.

I promised her I would *never* race again, and she promised she would never *dance* again, but *I* couldn't keep my promise because racing gets in your blood, like corpuscles, and I just *had* to race, just one more time, at Indianapolis. I guess I shouldn't have done it just this one more time, but as it turned out, I finished first and won a hundred and thirty-six thousand dollars and a lifetime supply of Allstate tires.

So that's why I say: Just before the head-on collision, Mother, I am thinking, dear, of you (you're all *Mother,* Mother). That's why I'm thinking, dear, of you.

14

Bongo, the Baby
Elephant
or
Never Turn Your Back
on a Motorcycle Race

BONGO, the baby elephant, weighed fourteen thousand pounds. Bongo knew how much he weighed because he went to the corner drugstore and weighed himself. The little card said: "You weigh fourteen thousand pounds, and you're going to meet a tall, dark, and handsome young man." This made Bongo smile because actually he wasn't too sure of himself.

It made the druggist smile, too. Although it couldn't be called a true smile. The druggist just *looked* like he was smiling, after Bongo accidentally stepped on him. Bongo wanted some chewing gum, but after looking at the druggist, he realized his desire could only lead to futility.

Bongo was quite different from most elephants. He was very intelligent and could also talk, if he wanted to. Although the only language he knew was Yugoslavian. A very difficult language to understand. And Bongo had a lisp, which made *his* Yugoslavian *very* difficult to understand. So much so that for a long time, nobody even knew he was an *elephant*. He tried to *explain* that he was an elephant to anybody who would listen, but nobody would listen. Then he tried explaining that he was Yugoslavian, but again nobody would listen. Then one day, in a saloon, he explained that he was a Yugoslavian *elephant*. This time, everybody *listened* to him, but nobody *believed* him. (You know how many phonies you run into in saloons.)

Then one day, Bongo ran into someone who believed him. Gregory Ratoff. He not only believed Bongo's story, he brought him to Hollywood and put him into the movies. Mr. Ratoff directed Bongo's first picture, *An Elephant Is a Many Splendored Thing*. It was a musical. With Ginger Rogers. Bongo and Ginger never did get along very well. Poor Ginger, she just couldn't seem to learn the dance routines.

Gossip had it that Bongo made them a little too difficult for her.

After this first picture, which was a smash, Bongo was the biggest thing in Hollywood and became increasingly more difficult with every day that passed. For one thing, he stubbornly refused to change his name to Tab or Rock or Lance. He pointed out that Telefunken Trefflich had never changed *his* name and *he* was doing all right. (Nobody ever *heard* of Telefunken Trefflich or what he was doing all right *at,* but one didn't argue too much with a big star like Bongo had become overnight.)

And Bongo really played the star role to the hilt. He had a forty-five room mansion in Beverly Hills, a hundred-foot swimming pool, a white Jaguar sports truck, and had become insecure.

There's nothing quite so insecure as an insecure elephant. He was so insecure he got married. To a starlet. At least, *he* thought she was a starlet (an elephant has very small eyes, you know). Actually Barbara-Jean Bagg *had* been a starlet back in the days when Mathew Brady was head cameraman, for D. W. Griffith's great-grandfather. She had also been a "Goldwyn girl" (sorry, Mrs. Goldwyn, but you would have found out sooner or later).

Bongo and his lovely wife were happy for a while (about a day and a half) then she went to Las Vegas for the usual reason—craps (and a divorce). She took poor Bongo for everything he had. The Beverly

Hills mansion. The swimming pool. The water. And fifty thousand dollars in cash that Bongo had stashed away. No one knew where Bongo had stashed it until one day he sneezed, in an unfortunate location (*her* lawyer's office).

Poor Bongo, he was brokenhearted and very discouraged. Nothing seemed to mean anything anymore. He didn't know where to turn or what to do. He began to think about going home. Going back to Africa, but he was afraid he'd run into Robert Ruark, and find himself a trophy, before he'd had a chance to explain that he was just a tourist (and an American citizen).

Daily his spirits drooped lower and lower. He didn't know anyone who would sell marijuana to an elephant, so he did the next best thing. He started to drink. Wine at first. He figured like everybody else—a few barrels of wine never hurt *any* elephant. Then, of course, he started to get less and less kick from the 12 per cent stuff and switched to *straight vodka!* He didn't mix it with *anything*. To hell with Commander Whitehead! If you wanna *get* someplace—*get* there!

Bongo drank secretly at first. Then openly. And it didn't take long for it to get around that he was rapidly developing into a fourteen-thousand-pound lush. Finally one day, some columnist ran one of those blind items: "*What* elephant showed up at *what* studio *what* morning with a *snootfull???*" Pretty subtle, huh?

Things went from bad to worse. He lost his job at the studio because he refused to do a remake of *Blue Angel*. (He thought his legs weren't right—besides he had *two too many* for the part.) *That* did it! Bongo was through!

After much maneuvering and finagling, Bongo's agent got him a singing engagement, in Las Vegas. Opening night he didn't show up. Sammy Davis, Junior, had to sub for him. Unfortunately, Sammy Davis, Junior, didn't show up either. Liberace showed up, but he had sequin poisoning and couldn't play.

Bongo was really on a toboggan slide now. Not only professionally, but socially. He was no longer invited to Marion Davies' parties. (Come to think of it—neither was *she*.) Everywhere he went, Jackie Coogan snubbed him. Jeff Chandler acted like he didn't know him. (Which really wasn't Jeff's fault—they'd never met.)

In show business, it doesn't take long before they forget you (even if you're a famous elephant). And poor Bongo was finding this out, the hard way. He appeared on "What's My Line?" and Dorothy Kilgallen didn't even come close!

He started drinking more heavily than ever before, but even in his rum-soaked brain he had an idea. If he could just find *another* elephant who drank, they could team up, and perhaps hire themselves out to some weird librarian who would be fascinated by the idea of drunken book ends. But this brilliant scheme never got beyond the planning stage, not that it was any task to find another alcoholic elephant, or a weird librarian, but before Bongo got beyond the first stages, *tragedy struck!* He got an offer for a television series. Be sure and watch your newspaper for the time and station. The series is called: *Frontier Elephant*.

If you follow the advice,
"If you drink, don't drive,"
how are you going to get home?

16

Foul-Up Freddie

Making Introductions

"Mr. and Mrs. Jones—I want you to meet Doctor Smith and his lovely wife, Imogene.

"What? You're not Doctor Smith, and this *isn't* your lovely wife, Imogene? Your name is Hammerslagg, and you're a plumber? Well, where *is* your wife? Oh I see—I'm sorry Mrs. Hammerslagg, I thought your name was Smith.

"When I saw you last night at Toots Shor's with Mr. Smith—I thought—

"Well—if you'll pardon me—I've got to get to the post office before the prices change!"

At a Party

"Quiet, everybody, we're going to play a grand party game—really grand—everybody know how to play—Tickle Tickle???? Nobody knows how to play Tickle Tickle? Well, let Uncle Freddie show you, you don't know what you've been missing! Now first— all the girls take off their shoes and stockings—that's it—now all the men take off their shoes and socks— that's it. Now, we take all the shoes and socks and stockings and we put them all together in this laundry bag. Now, all the boys on one side of the room, all the girls on the other side. Now we put out all the lights. And now we—now, wait a minute—what do we do now? Don't get excited! Quiet! I'm trying to think! Oh, I know! No, that's a different game. Say, I've got an idea—let's eat!"

* * *

Watching Television

"Must be a poor director on this TV show, I just saw the shadow of the boom microphone. It made that one guy look like he's wearing a hat. Huh? Oh, yeah, it's a black derby. Well, it *looked* like a shadow.

"That's the actor I was reading about. He's been married ten times—or he has ten children—one of the two.

"This plot is paper thin. I could tell five minutes

ago she wouldn't shoot her husband. The motivation is all wrong—you can tell.

"Ooops, she shot him, didn't she? Well, that's not the way I'd have written it.

"But what can you expect from show business, they're all a little abnormal, you know. A friend of mine is in show business and he told me—he's an usher at the Palace.

"Your set looks a little out of sync, there—don't worry—I'll fix it. There are several buttons here on the back that most folks don't know about. Let's turn this one, how's that? No picture, huh??? Well, I'll turn this other one. How's that? No sound, huh???

"Well, here's the button I was looking for. There! How's that? The light's gone out, huh?"

17

Jackie Gleason—Unite!

18

Over the Fence

"Hi, neighbor—nice to see you around after last night. I didn't think you'd make it. What do I mean? Oh, nothing, but kicking that poor cop—especially after he was nice enough to bring you home.

"No, no, you weren't making much noise—you quieted right down. Right after they wrapped you in that wet sheet.

"Oh, I wouldn't worry about your wife. She didn't get home until a couple of hours later. She came home in her Cadillac. What? She doesn't have a Cadillac? Oh, yes, come to think of it, when she kissed her brother good night—he drove it away.

"What? She doesn't have a brother, either? Well—I wouldn't worry, it was a very short kiss—not more than twenty minutes.

"She looked kinda cute—standing there on the porch—in her bathing suit. Don't see many bikinis around here.

"How's your son—the one that's in the service? You know, I didn't know he was Japanese—he's not? You mean he's in *our* army?!

"How's your darling daughter—I haven't read the papers lately—did she get back from that Mediterranean cruise yet? Well, I'll bet she's having a wonderful time—those oil tankers are lots of fun.

"But I must say your place is looking wonderful—you're quite a gardener. You really have a green thumb. Yes, sir, that's what you have, a green thumb —just too bad it's spreading.

"But I really, just between us, think your place would look a lot nicer if you could put your car in your garage. But, of course, I guess there isn't much room, what with your *still,* and all— And those alcohol fumes aren't too bad—of course, our dog comes home drunk every day—but that's his own fault—he sniffs a lot. But of course, he's not the only one who sniffs—those Federal men have pretty good noses, too.

"Oh, don't be silly—I would never tell anyone that you're making moonshine—what do you think I am—a stool pigeon? Say, how do you like my new power mower? How much? Well, it really didn't cost me anything—I used the reward money.

"Say, I wonder if you'd check my gas meter one of these days. I think I'm being overcharged. Why should you know how to check a gas meter? Well— I've seen you checking yours—at least you were doing something with that long-handled screw driver.

"Oh, I wouldn't think of saying anything to Charlie. Who's Charlie? He's my brother-in-law. He's the meter reader for this district. But I wouldn't say anything to him. It wouldn't be neighborly. I want to be good neighbors, that's why I refused when he asked me to sneak up on you with the summons.

"No, no, I don't mind the smoke from your incinerator. Does have a funny smell though, doesn't it? That last batch of five-dollar bills didn't turn out so good did they?

"Well—wadda you care—the tens are perfect.

"No—I don't mind if your chickens come over on my side of the fence and scratch up my garden— I don't mind at all—and besides—we were going to buy a bigger deep freeze anyway.

"No, I have no complaints at all—I think you are a very good neighbor—that's why I wouldn't sign the petition.

"What petition? Oh, it's nothing—everybody in the neighborhood signed it—but believe me, it's nothing. And besides—why should someone be censured *all* his life for something he did *thirty years ago*.

"I studied the case thoroughly—there was plenty reasonable doubt that you killed your beautiful blond secretary at the office Christmas party because she was blackmailing you.

"Just because she was lying on the floor with a bullet hole in her and you were standing over her with a smoking revolver in your hand doesn't mean that *you* did it!

"It could have been the window cleaner—but of course he wasn't working that day.

"And it could have been the cleaning woman—you know—jealousy.

"I'm very glad that you got out of it okay—because I believed in you—I believed in you from the very moment that Clarence Darrow said he would take your case.

"Well—have a pleasant day."

19

Remember . . . ?

When you didn't have to be tattooed to smoke a cigarette?

When a couch was used for *making* love—instead of *telling* about it?

When we had sunny weekends?

"Get well" cards that meant it?

Movies in which some of the actors were still alive?

When every girl bumped off in a hotel room wasn't an actress or a model?

20

Although It's Only Make-Believe, Laugh, String, Laugh

(An American Failure Story)

THERE ONCE was a piece of string that wanted to be a rope. That was the one thing that this little piece of string wanted the most. And he was willing to do anything to achieve this worthy (to him) ambition. But, unfortunately, this piece of string was stupid (even for a piece of string), and he didn't know how to go about becoming a rope. He read all the ads in the cheap magazines, and according to them you could be anything you wanted to be, from a taxidermist in your spare time, to potent—at any time. All you had to do was clip the coupon. But there were no ads on how to become a rope, if you were just a piece of string. Ralf, which was this particular piece of string's name, got more than a little desperate. There was so little time, when you were nothing but a piece of string. At any moment he expected to be tied around a package and shipped out to God-knows-where. He didn't want this to happen. Oh how he didn't want this to happen! Because even though he was only a piece of string he had all the emotions of a rope. He had known love, hate, frustration, and Char Shu Ding, which is diced roast pork, bamboo shoots, water chestnuts, and fried rice, and sometimes used as a substitute for love, hate, and frustration in some of the better suburban communities. Of course, in a couple of hours, you're loved, hated, and frustrated all over again. (But one thing at a time—and our immediate problem is this piece of string which, or is it who, wants to become a rope.)

Many years passed and the piece of string was no nearer his goal. He just couldn't seem to learn the secret. He watched ropes every chance he got (he became sort of a sisal voyeur), but the trick eluded him. Finally he went to the Ford Foundation and stated his problem simply and honestly:

"Kids, I am goddam sick and tired of being a piece of string. I wanna be a rope!"

The Ford Foundation people looked at each other, fighting for control.

"Why do you wanna become a rope?" asked one of the Ford people (the one with guts).

"Look—I didn't come here to answer a lot of stupid questions. Are you gonna help me or not?" replied the piece of string (who had a lot of guts himself, when you come to think of it).

"Okay," said the paymaster of the Ford group, "here's a check for ten thousand dollars—spend it wisely."

And the piece of string did spend the ten thousand dollars wisely, strange to say. He went out and took rope lessons. He took rope lessons for almost fifteen years, at the Rope Institute of America. Actually he never learned to become a rope, but for a while there he was really living, which is about all you can expect if you're a piece of string—with no connections.

Warning

If you get three tickets in a row for jaywalking, they take away your legs.

22

School Days

Pudge Winthrop was the richest kid in school—
he was so rich he had jockeys for his saddle shoes.
He also had his own French maid and his own golf
course to chase her over. The silver spoon in his
mouth—made him very difficult to understand. And
he didn't just subscribe to *Playboy*. Once a month
they'd send up the girls. That was his ambition in
life: to be an international playboy like Rubirosa
says he used to be. In fact, he was the one voted
the most likely to meet Linda Christian.

Of course, it didn't work out that way. Pudge
lost all his money, and the last time I saw him he

was working as a window tapper in a drive-in movie. That's the guy that goes around tapping on car windows and saying: "Ah! Ah! Ah! Ah!"

Then there was Herbie Floomp. He was the best-dressed guy in school. That is, he wasn't exactly the best-dressed guy, he just happened to have argyle hair on his legs.

The school's aim was to teach us how to be men, which really wasn't very hard, because we were all *boys* to start with. Right next door there was a girls' school, surrounded by an eight foot stone wall with a hot wire and broken bottles on the top of it. We didn't mind the hot wire—but we never did find a way to short out those broken bottles.

I had two good chums in school. We went everywhere together, and everybody used to call us The Three Musketeers until they got wise, after which we were known as The Purple Gang.

find your next big pay boost here...➡

Just mark your name and field of interest on the attached coupon and mail it to I.C.S. You'll receive absolutely FREE a valuable Career Kit with 3 famous books that have helped thousands on the way to a better job, bigger pay! . . . (see other side).

FREE I.C.S. CAREER KIT
SHOWS YOU CAN GET AHEAD

1 **"How to Succeed"** is a gold mine of tips on how your personality, your outlook on life can affect your future. It will help you discover hidden talents in yourself, show how to plan your career, how to deal with your boss, how to choose your goals. Plus dozens of other ideas on how you can succeed.

2 **"Opportunity Catalog"** is a complete job directory that outlines opportunities in the field that interests you most. It gives you down-to-earth facts on just what you can expect and what your chances are for success in the career you choose.

3 **"Sample I.C.S. Lesson"** (math) demonstrates the famous method by which so many people have achieved success. Literally thousands upon thousands of men and women of all ages have won promotions, security and better pay through I.C.S. training. And you can do the same. Mail the prepaid, self-addressed postcard today.

The Golden Book
of Sex

"BUT, HERBERT—looking back, it seems to me, there *must* be an *easier* way to die than just *living!*"—"Please don't look at me that way, Mother. I *had* to shoot you. This is *your* day!"—"But *why* does it always have to be this way, Miss Kwoon? *Why* must we live *lives* of *quiet desperation?* What's wrong with *A Party without* Betty Comden and Adolf Green?"

These fascinating sentences are culled from a new children's book by Charles Dickens. Where he *mailed* it from heaven only knows. The book is rather reminiscent of *Lolita* and *Black Beauty* with a dash of Mary

Astor's *first* (and best) diary. Incidentally *Lolita*, in case you haven't heard, is being made into a movie. They've switched the idea around somewhat. As it stands now, Mae West and Roddy McDowall are playing the two leading roles.

This book, *The Golden Book of Sex*, is being highly recommended by Gayelord Hauser, mainly I feel, because the cover is green. Mr. Hauser may take umbrage at this, but I don't care anymore, and while I think of it, Mr. Hauser, since I cut out polly seeds my voice is much lower (and so is my perch).

Nevertheless, getting back to this teeny tome for tiny tots, I think it's Caryl Chessman's best, and I would like to add my endorsement, because I feel that giving any book to a child is a step in the right direction, because some of the toys today are not only non-educational but very sharp-edged and your child is liable to cut himself while he's slashing you. I have never given *my* child toys. When he was very young I used to give him "model" kits, and he used to spend most of his playtime building models. Of course, they only lived for a few minutes, but—

This book would make an ideal birthday or Christmas gift for any boy or girl, regardless of sex.

Lady Chatterley's daughter whose name is Lambretta (she conceived on an Italian scooter) is giving a party to welcome her lover, Cantinflas Gleckle, a famous Spanish bullfighter, who arrives at the party in an ambulance because he had been gored only the day before, while taking bows, in the bull ring at Madrid, by a bull who had turned out to be a remarkably good actor. (*Everybody* thought he was dead!)

"Welcome to Windy Poplars, Señor Gleckle!" murmured the lovely Lambretta, as she lazily lit a cigarette from the tiny blue flame that burned eternally in her navel (in honor of her own, private memory of the Boer War).

"Buenos días, mi bonita Lambretta," shouted Señor Gleckle as he eased himself onto the tomato aspic ottoman that Lambretta had so thoughtfully provided for his temporary tenderment.

"I have bad news, my lover," said Señor Gleckle.

"How wonderful," replied Lambretta.

"I must go back to my people—*tonight!*"

"But you can't go back! You can't go back to the reservation and live like a common savage!" screamed Lambretta.

"You forget, my dear," said Señor Gleckle, drawing himself to his full height. "*I* am a *Sioux!*"

"Give it up!"

"Give up—being a Sioux?"

"Yes, if you *love* me!"

After a moment of quiet meditation he moved toward her, tomahawk in hand.

Every child should read: *The Golden Book of Sex.* If for no other reason.

CHAPTER
24

Drums

IT'S COMMON knowledge that drums were one of the earliest forms of communication. Drums have always been famous—especially in history. The expression "Tight as a drum" was coined during the Civil War. One of General Grant's aides said it.

There were a lot of drummer boys in the Civil War. As a matter of fact, my great-great-grandfather was one. I still have his old drum at home—it's full of holes. They're not bullet holes, he just played with very sharp sticks.

The drummer boy in that picture, "The Spirit of '76," is my great-great-great-great-grandfather. The guy next to him with his head bandaged isn't wounded, he's just trying to keep out the sound of the drum.

25

The Third Oldest Profession

IT'S TRUE, there is *no* business like *show* business. The Standard Oil Company! General Motors! General Foods! Procter & Gamble! What do *they* know? Why don't they wise up, and get into *show* business, where the *real* money is?

There are *no* folks like *show* folks! They're true-blue. They'll stick with you to the *end!* They'll even help you *plan* it.

And no matter what personal tragedy may strike their own private lives, you'd never know it to look at them, because they always have a smile on their lips. Because they're idiots.

The show must go on. That's what they believe. Even after they've read the reviews. But no one can deny that grease paint gets into your blood. Actually, according to the American Medical Association, it *doesn't*, but it *does* get all over your collar, and this seems to have a narcotic effect, especially on the young. They all dream of someday becoming Tony Perkins. (Incidentally, have you ever *seen* Tony Perkins? His wrists are *thirty-five inches long*. Uncanny.)

There is a strange fascination about show business for all of us. And there have been great moments in the theater. Moments when the world seemed to stand still for an instant. Like that magical moment when for the first time, the great Blossom Krinebine and the great Benny Farfel stepped into the golden spotlight on the stage of the old Palace Theater and couldn't remember the lyrics to their opening song. That was a night the stardust hit the fan.

And what Broadwayite could ever forget another magical moment, that thrilling opening night at the old Amsterdam roof, when lovely "Twinkletoes" Feen danced too near the edge, and fell thirty-two stories to the pavement of Old Broadway. A *magical* moment indeed! Messy, but magical.

Then there was the immortal "Lady Gay" belting her heart out, standing there in that green overhead spotlight singing: "Happiness is a thing called Pod." Poor "Lady Gay," she's gone now. She accidentally slipped through a crack in an old player piano and was felt-hammered to death.

More recently of course, was Ralf "Blue-Bottle-Fly" Gleckle, the famous Espresso Parlor folk singer. His great talent has been stilled by his inner torment, having committed suicide in 1938 by washing his turtleneck sweater in warm water, then putting it on wet. The headline in *Variety* read: "Punk's Trunk Shrunk in Funk."

Then there was old Bix. Bix Gleckle, the greatest cornet player of them all. Bix could blow so high and so loud, if you stood within twenty feet of him your eyes would bleed. The first time he played at Carnegie Hall, the first three rows were beheaded. And the rest of the crowd left the hall with long pointed ears with tiny tassels on the ends of them. His horn got so hot he had to use tongs. But old Bix fell on evil days. It all started when he was arrested one night in Birdland. For being a Flamingo. (For you fortunate people who don't live in New York, it should be explained "Birdland" is not for the birds—it's for the cats.)

Even though some of Broadway's brightest stars are gone. Broadway is *still* Broadway. With its hundreds of sparkling fruit juice stands. Its many captivating, multicolored signs, advertising such fascinating divertissements as "Hygrade All-Meat Frankfurters," "Robert Hall Clothes," and "This Space for Rent." Broadway with its Gaiety (it's a delicatessen). Broadway with its carefree laughter (a recording). Broadway with its inlaid chewing gum sidewalks. Its wall-to-wall drunks. Its charming pickpockets, its titivating muggers, and its trips to Chinatown (and if you go with the wrong girl, you'll probably wind up in downtown Hong Kong). (Minus the gold watch your father gave you for not using cocaine before you were twenty-one.)

Yes, Broadway *is* still Broadway, and as that great Broadway showman, George M. Gleckle, once said, as he was drinking champagne out of Lillian Russell's slipper: "Madam, if your feet were as big as your heart, I'd be loaded!"

CHAPTER
26

The Wonderful World of Narcotics

NARCOTICS are habit-forming, which is, of course, the most wonderful thing of all about them. There are many kinds of narcotics. Narcotics that make you sleep, narcotics that keep you awake, narcotics that teach you to dance. Invented by a group who are trying to stamp out Arthur Murray (a worthy, if losing cause). "H" or heroin, which was brought to the attention of the world by the combined efforts of the Federal Bureau of Narcotics and the Mafia, is probably the most popular brand of dope. Mainly because it can be transported so easily (apparently) and because a little bit of heroin goes a long, long way.

(Hasn't anyone thought of *this* as a song title?) "A little bit of heroin goes a long, long way, 'cause my mother came from there."

From heroin can be made cocaine—which can be sniffed or needled or just served over the rocks (with opium canapés). Which is actually the best and most conspicuous way of serving it. This chapter sounds like a defense of the use of narcotics, doesn't it? Well, it is.

Let us think back to all the greats of history. How about Edgar Allan Poe—could he have written *War and Peace* without the use of narcotics? I think not. And how about Tolstoy—without the right needle in the right vein I doubt very much if he would have ever gone near a piano and "Suwanee River" and "The Old Folks at Home" would have been lost to the world.

From what I understand, the beat generation, who are, of course, better known as "the people who *don't* use Dial soap, and don't you wish they did?" generation, are quite addicted to addiction. There is something about this that I really don't understand, because apparently this particular group does no work of any kind, and in order to become at least a halfway respectable hophead you must have money to buy it. Now—where does the beat generation get the money to buy dope? Is some Foundation stretching a point in their behalf? Could be. Maybe I haven't read *all* the papers lately. Maybe there *is* a Nobel prize for Hasheesh. Or maybe Pulitzer has ceased to care about literary efforts and switched to fun! fun! fun!

I have tried marijuana, myself. I was about a year and a half old and mother had left me at this nursery while she went shopping and some of the other kids who were a little older (about two) were smoking it, and I didn't want to be a bum sport so *I* tried it. I loved it. The only trouble was, from that day on mother's milk made me sick. I just couldn't face those things without a little pod first. (Pod is hip talk for Mexican filter-tips.)

There are a few rules about the use of dope which I think one should follow if one is to play the game. Firstly, one should never smoke weed in bed. One is liable to fall asleep and burn one—or two or three or four—depends on how many in your party.

Secondly, never whip out an opium cooker and your pipe on a crowded bus. Firstly, someone is liable to jostle your cooker and put the flame out. And secondly, no matter how many times you explain to the other people on the bus that it's not an opium pipe—it's a flute and the cooker is a flute warmer, and you're on your way to play a concert at Carnegie Hall with a full explanation by Leonard Bernstein—it would be much better if Leonard Bernstein were with you on the bus, where an explanation might be really needed.

The thirdly rule is a rule which should never be broken under any circumstance; if you want to try heroin, or cocaine, or opium, or marijuana, I have a suggestion. Don't try them all together. Or better still, *do* try them all at the same time, and if you get in trouble, call the automobile club, they'll have moon maps, I'm sure.

Famous Quotes
or What
They Were Really Doing

"THIS is going to hurt me more than it hurts you."

Father, who's just found out his son is carrying a blackjack.

.   .   .

"But, Baby, it's cold outside!"

It was at Valley Forge, she was a friend of George's —and she *wasn't* giving a weather report.

"We don't know where our next meal is coming from."

The man was telling the truth—he had a cross-eyed cook.

.   .   .

"It's only a shanty in old shantytown."

The man had made the last payment on the G.I. house he bought right after the war.

.   .   .

"Dig We Must."

A visitor to Birdland, trying to understand the music.

.   .   .

"I shall return."

It was payday at Remington Rand, and General MacArthur was coming back later to pick up his check.

"Four" Is a Four-Letter Word

"Espresso Is Thicker Than Water"

By Tennessee Gleckle *

(A pantomime with words, to be played on a bare stage without actors.)

The music: Progressive silence.
The lighting: The theater is on fire.
The curtain does not rise—it is torn to shreds by the audience.
After an impressive forty-five-minute pause, Mildred speaks.

MILDRED.
You're *scared*, Roger. That's *your* trouble. Deep down inside you're *scared!*

---

* Watch for his new Columbia LP album: "Bitch with Mitch."

ROGER.

Don't say that, Mildred. Don't say it! *Please don't say I'm scared!*

MILDRED.

Roger, baby, there's nothing wrong with being scared. *Everybody's* scared. The cop on the beat is scared. The man on the street is scared. The butcher, the baker, the candlestick maker . . . they're *all scared!*

ROGER.

Is the Old *Hootie Owl* scared?

MILDRED.

Scared *hoot*-less!

ROGER.

Is . . . Buster Crabbe scared?

MILDRED.

What's the matter, Roger, aren't things going right at the Laundromat?

ROGER.

It's not that, Mildred. It's just that I feel I must paint.

MILDRED.

You mean give up your wife and children, and your business, and go to Tahiti and *paint?*

ROGER.

Yes . . . but . . . *how* did you *know?*

MILDRED.

I saw it last night on the "The Late Show."

ROGER.

Did you watch "The Shirley Temple Storybook"?

MILDRED.

Yeah.

ROGER.

I think the butler did it.

MILDRED.

Did you watch Alfred Hitchcock?

ROGER.

Yeah. I think Shirley Temple did it.

MILDRED.

Roger, you *know* something.

ROGER.

It ain't that, Mildred. It's just that I don't trust that Shirley Temple.

MILDRED.

You're right, Roger, you turn your back on that Shirley Temple and zunk! Right between the shoulder blades!

ROGER.

Now hold on there, Mildred! How *dare* you say things like that about Shirley!

MILDRED.

Aw! They're all alike, them movie stars. Puffed-up sweaters with nothin' behind them!

ROGER.

You're bitter, Mildred. *Very bitter.*

MILDRED.

Why shouldn't I be bitter? Fourteen years a nurse's aid, and *not once* have they asked me to operate! Why? Why? Why?

ROGER.

Your hands are dirty.

MILDRED.

That makes sense.

ROGER.

Sure it does.

MILDRED.

Give me a reasonable answer and I'm not bitter anymore . . . when's her birthday?

ROGER.

Whose?

MILDRED.

Shirley Temple's. I'm gonna bake her a midget.

ROGER.

Mildred . . . you're *all* heart.

MILDRED.

Yeah.

CURTAIN

Winners of the 1960 Fortune
Cooky Writers' Contest

"Merry Xmas and a Happy Egg Foo Yung"

"Number One on Chinese Hit Parade: 'The Night
We Got High, by the River Kwai, and Your Mother
Fell off the Bridge' "

"No Chinese Fortune today—Chinese office party
last night"

"Your baby sitter has just driven your car through
the Holland Tunnel, and is headed West"

"Your baby sitter has just bitten your baby"

CHAPTER

31

All You Can Eat for
Two Hundred Dollars
or
Sell Your Sister and
Have Dinner Out
Tonight

LAST SPRING, while I was lying in the hospital, recovering from a very serious operation (they have surgery for hangovers now, you know), a friend of mine who happens to do public relations for a group known as Restaurant Associates, sent me a forty-five-course Roman-type, orgy-style dinner from a new restaurant called The Forum of the Twelve Caesars. I was very grateful to them, but goddamned annoyed at my nurse because she wouldn't serve me in the nude. To the waist, that was as far as she'd go.

But when I saw Miss Krine standing there, in what she mistook for *all her glory,* the real significance behind the phrase "a motley group" struck home.

Nevertheless the food was fabulously exotic, rare, and expensive, as I found out when I later dined at the restaurant itself, the walls of which are covered by a red silky fabric, and spaced at more or less regular intervals are twelve huge sixteenth century portraits of the twelve Caesars.

The menu itself is on the best-seller list, and the way it looks at present, the paperback edition won't be out for years. Here are a few (actually *very* few) choice samples from this fascinating publication:

SHELL-BORNE OUT OF THE SEA
Oysters and Pink Caviar.
Alban Crabmeat Set in Avocado Coronet.
The Oysters of Hercules.
A Tribute to Triton.

❧❧

MUSHROOM AND TRUFFLES
Great Mushrooms Stuffed with Snails,
Gallic Cheese, and Walnuts, Glazed.

A HARVEST FROM THE SEAS AND RIVERS
An Ocean Perch Aflame on Rosemary Herbs,
Lemon Ginger Sauce.
Lobster Jupiter, Poached in Herbs and Wine,
Served with "Olympian" Butter.

❖❖

SUMPTUOUS DISHES FROM ALL THE EMPIRE
Leg of Baby Lamb, Charcoal Roasted—
Sauce of Two Lively Lilies.

❖❖

EPICUREAN TROPHIES OF THE HUNT
Cutlet of Wild Boar Deviled in Mustard Seed,
Croutons, and Apple Nuggets.

❖❖

PLEASURES FROM THE IMPERIAL TABLE— CHARCOAL BROILED ON THE GLOWING HEARTH
Filet Mignon, Caesar Augustus, with a Rising
Crown of Pâté, and Triumphal Laurel Wreath.

*   *   *

The success of The Forum of the Twelve Caesars has inspired many imitators. The nearest is a restaurant formerly called "Joe's," which now flaunts the name, The Backroom of the Thirteen Nudnicks, and I say "flaunts" because it's right next door to The Forum of the Twelve Caesars, and they've copied everything—as closely as their more limited budget allows them.

The walls of The Backroom of the Thirteen Nudnicks are covered with a silky (more or less) red cheesecloth. Spaced at regular intervals are portraits of the Thirteen Nudnicks. There were supposed to be portraits of *fourteen* Nudnicks, but the Nudnick who was painting the portraits of the Nudnicks ran out of Nudnick paint. (It's a special kind of paint, smuggled into New York by wet-backs from New Jersey.) (They have it pumped directly into their blood, then when they arrive safely in New York, they're drained.) Incidentally, for those of you who don't know what a Nudnick is—a Nudnick is a Nebbish with a front tooth missing.

The menu of The Backroom of the Thirteen Nudnicks is a direct plagiarism changed only slightly to avoid a lawsuit:

SHELL-BORNE OUT OF FLUSHING BAY
Pink Lox on Beige Bagel.
Flounder Fins on Flaming Chicken Feathers.
Unborn Crabmeat Thrown into an Electric Fan—
Served with Baked Bathtowels.

MUSHROOMS, TRUFFLES, BANGLES, BAUBLES, AND BEADS
Snails Stuffed with Snails Stuffed with Snails.
Oklahoma Sardines with Chopped Rubber Boot.

❧❧

HARVEST FROM THE FULTON FISH MARKET AND OTHER FUN PLACES
Salmon Tongues on Crabgrass—
with Sauce Bénzadréné.

❧❧

EPICUREAN TROPHIES OF THE HUNT
Braised Petal of Ubangi Lip.
Mustang Muscatel.

❧❧

SUMPTUOUS DISHES FROM ALL OF THE A & P
Baked Beans à la Solitude.
(Note: Each individual bean is wrapped in cellophane, and baked for three years deep down in the Carlsbad Caverns—don't plan on the theater if you order this dish.)

❧❧

CHARCOAL BROILED FROM THE GLOWING COOK
Filet of Camel Hump—on a Rising Arab—
Crowned with a Flaming Brush Fire—
and Served by a Singed Waiter.

New York has many wonderful restaurants, like the fabulous new Four Seasons (the place with the nervous curtains), but I personally prefer a nice frozen TV Dinner at home, mainly because it's so little trouble. All you have to do is have another drink, while you're throwing it in the garbage.

32

Monday

DEAR DIARY: I saw Mildred today. She was coming out of the Stork Club wearing a mink coat and a big diamond ring and she was with a guy. You know what *I* think, Dear Diary? I think it's *all over* between Mildred and me.

33

Tuesday

DEAR DIARY: I saw Mildred again today. She was coming out of the Stork Club wearing two mink coats and three diamond rings and she was with five guys and Georgie Jessel. You know what *I* think, Dear Diary? I think Mildred is playing around.

CHAPTER
34

Wednesday

DEAR DIARY: Saw Mildred again today. She was coming out of the Stork Club wearing a diamond coat, sapphire slacks and she was with the Milwaukee Braves. You know what I think, Dear Diary? I think Mildred is trying to make the cover of *Sports Illustrated*. But *what* sport?

CHAPTER
35

Thursday

DEAR DIARY: I waited in front of the Stork Club all day today, but I didn't see Mildred come out. She didn't come out yesterday, either. Or the day before that. You know, Dear Diary—it's been a long time since I've seen Mildred come out of the Stork Club. Almost *six years*.

CHAPTER
36

Friday

DEAR DIARY: I saw Mildred come out today. Not out of the Stork Club. I saw her come out of a hospital on Eighth Avenue, with the Milwaukee Braves and the Harlem Globetrotters. They were all carrying babies. You know what I think, Dear Diary? I think Mildred's got it made. I mean the cover of *Sports Illustrated*.

37

*The Abominable
Snowman
or
Mother Had the Biggest
Feet in Town and Oh,
What Fun She Had in
the Wintertime in Tibet*

TIBET is an Asiatic country, containing Mount Everest, which is a famous off-Broadway lump. Tibet is located a helluva long way from downtown Detroit, which is the main reason you don't see many Edsels (in downtown Tibet).

Tibet first became known to the Western world when Ronald Colman made a movie about it called

Lost Horizon in which Ronald tried to smuggle a beautiful young girl out of the country, but on the way she turned into a wrinkled old hag. I don't remember whether it was because it was a long trip, or this supposedly beautiful girl had had a face job and the altitude had made the whole thing slip. She later became a strip teaser on 52nd Street under the name of "Wrinkles" Randall. "Wrinkles" did a very exotic and unique act. While the band played "A Pretty Girl Is Like a Melody" she used to iron herself out.

The mating season is very short in Tibet. Mainly because the population is all male. (If there are any questions about this, please be brief and enclose a crisp dollar bill.)

The Giant Panda is a native of Tibet. The Giant Panda lives in bamboo thickets and feeds on bamboo shoots. There are only thirty-six Giant Pandas left, according to Sir Hillary Brook, who has hunted big game all over the world. (He once shot a Rhino in St. Louis at a New Year's Eve party.) The reason there are only thirty-six Giant Pandas left, explains Sir Hillary, is the shortage of bamboo shoots, which the natives eat in great quantities, especially with baked Giant Panda.

Tibet is the *highest* country in the world (they have to keep warm *somehow!*). And it is bounded on the north by Sinkiang, on the northeast by the Chinese province of Chinghai, on the east by the Chinese province of Sikang, on the west by Kashmir and Ladakh, and on the south by India, Nepal, Bhutan, and Los Angeles.

Tibet is inhabited mainly by Tibetans (where *else* could they go in them crazy outfits?). And the country, until recently, was ruled by the Dalai Lama, who was elected when he was five years old and whose real name is Lingerh Lamutanchu, which is also the name of a small Tibetan sports car (made out of Yak milk).

Monogamy, polygamy, polyandry, and volley ball are all practiced in Tibet, especially the first. Polygamy is practiced among those whose wealth suffices to support more than one wife. Polyandry is practiced among the herdsmen and the farmers. Actually, volley ball isn't practiced in Tibet any more because somebody stole the net.

And so, as the sun sinks slowly behind the Lhasa-Hilton, we climb upon our wild asses (sounds like yogi, doesn't it?) and head back to civilization. Farewell, Mount Everest. Farewell, Dalai Lama. Farewell, Giant Panda and Yak. Farewell, Monogamy, Polygamy, Polyandry, and Volley Ball. And last but not least, Farewell, Abominable Snowman. Don't call *us*, we'll call *you*.

38

*The Hollywood
Funeral
or
Getting There Is Half
the Fun
or
Death Is Just a Bowl of
Cherries*

A FRIEND of mine, Ralf Krine, had been a Hollywood disc jockey. I say "had been" because he was now dead. Or as they say in California: "He had gone to that big Palm-Springs-in-the-Sky." Ralf made lots of friends while he was alive. He was that kind of a guy. But now that he was dead, somehow his gregariousness died with him. I had to take charge of all the arrangements, mainly because his relatives preferred to remain anonymous. Having participated in a few Hollywood funerals as an *honorary* pallbearer, which means you don't have to *lift*. You just have to be there (for the newsreels).

A Hollywood funeral is designed for fun! fun! fun! First you pick out a real hip casket (with the corners rounded off), then you pick out the choreographer, whose services, if he's good, will cost in the neighborhood of about three hundred dollars. Of course, for this, you won't get no Jack Cole or Jerry Robbins or Michael Kidd. But you'll get some "pretty good" movement, which is actually all that counts. Once this is done, you're half way home, or more correctly, the deceased is.

Picking the right cemetery can be a problem. There are so many in and around Hollywood. Of course, the word "cemetery" is never used. In Hollywood, a "cemetery" becomes a supereuphemism like: "Bye-Bye-Land," "No-play-Land," "Endsville-Land," and "Tomorrow-Land" (for true believers only). There is something else that you have to think of when picking the right last resting place, and that's the *entertainment* (no 20 per cent tax here). Most of the newer places have Muzak, and if you want to invest a few more dollars, you can choose one that features a Lester Lanin group, or Xavier Cugat, without Abbe, of course.

(There'd be too much getting up and dancing going on, they figure.)

Now let's consider, as I had to do for my late friend, Ralf Krine, what kind of services do we want?

In this department, you can run the gamut from a lay preacher with two hummingbirds (humming something appropriate) to Aimee Semple McGraham, the Hall-Johnson choir, and the chorus from *Can-Can*.

What about costume, I hear someone ask? Cecil Beaton, of course. If we can't have Cecil (he *is* terribly busy these days what with photographing the Queen and running guns into Cuba), we'll use Edith Head, or Don Loper or *any*one whom we can trust to do the right thing by Ralfie boy. And the right thing for a Hollywood funeral is, of course, Bermuda shorts, sandals, and naturally, the tennis racket tightly clenched in the right hand. Bad taste, you say? Nonsense! The *Pharaohs* were buried with *their* hobbies. (Hundreds of female skeletons were found in their tombs.)

* * *

Some time has passed since writing the first part of this chapter. Old Ralfie has been laid away for almost two weeks now, and just between us, things didn't go as we had planned. The honorary pallbearers didn't show up, so we had to use some old World War I movies for the newsreels. (Kinda made everybody wonder what the hell Kaiser Wilhelm and the Queen of Rumania were doing at a lousy disc jockey's funeral!) Then we couldn't get the choreographer we wanted so there was very little precision head bowing. And the cemetery was *all* wrong. No indirect lighting. No Espresso. No folk singers. No stereo. And what an inopportune time for a sports car race! (And I'm positive the judges were wrong. I'm sure the hearse was second and not third.)

Actually, it was probably the worst egg that was ever laid at "Bye-Bye-Land," the funeral, I mean. In fact, it was such a mish-mash, even Old Ralfie complained. I got a collect wire from him the next day. It said: "Thanks for everything, but next time (if there *is* a next time), may I have a little less talk and more music?"

39

Famous Misquotes

or

What They Really *Said*

ALL THROUGH the ages people have been misquoted. For instance the Dead Sea Scrolls—they were nothing like the Book. The incident at Bunker Hill is of course the most flagrant example of misquotation. Most of us know that the battle took place, not on Bunker, but on Breed's Hill, but what most of us don't know is what the American commanding officer said to his troops. He definitely did *not* say: "Don't fire until you see the whites of their eyes!" What he *actually* said was: "If it moves—shoot it, if it doesn't move—paint it!" Right, Vets?

After John Wilkes Booth jumped from where he had just shot Lincoln, to the stage of Ford's Theatre, he did *not* turn to the audience and shout: "Death to tyrants!" What he *did* say was, "I also have a shooting box in Scotland."

Another famous figure in American history who has been badly misquoted is Thomas Jefferson, who at that historic meeting in Philadelphia did *not* say: "If we don't hang together, we shall hang separately." What he *did* say, was: "For Crissakes—let's don't no-body sell 'em any rope!"

During the crucial naval battle on Lake Erie, Stephen Decatur did not say: "Don't give up the ship!" What he *did* say, was: "Don't give up the ship, because it's a helluva swim to the beach!"

Patrick Henry did *not* say: "Give me Liberty or give me Death!" What he *did* say was: "I don't know about the rest of you guys, but these tight colonial pants are killing me!"

Horace Greeley did *not* say: "Go West, Young Man." He said: "It's the first door on the left, Kid."

Shakespeare did *not* say: "All the world's a stage, and all the men and women merely players." What he *did* say, was: "The world is full of lousy actors!"

And that day in the Philippines, General MacArthur did *not* say: "I shall return!" What he *did* say, was: "Mind the store."

When Caesar was stabbed by Brutus he did *not* say:

"Et tu, Brute?" He said: "Brutus—just for that—no television tonight!"

Nobody actually knows what Custer said when he suddenly found himself and his group surrounded by thousands of screaming, bloodthirsty savages, but I have it on good authority that he turned to his aide and murmured: "I can't understand it—they were friendly enough last night at the dance."

40

"I Dreamed I Was the Statue of Liberty in My Maidenform Bra"
or
"Give Me Your Tired, Your Poor, Your Huddled Masses . . ."

BACK in the year 1680 François de la Rochefoucauld, the great maxim maker, said: "What a waste of good skin—giving breasts to women." Rochefoucauld also said: "Roses are red, Violets are blue. Sugar is sweet and so to bed." After having read Rochefoucauld over and over again, I still haven't figured out whether he was a maximist or a sex fiend. Or both. Might be a good combination.

One day, quite some time ago, I was lunching with the three Kahns (Gus, Genghis, and Sammy) and somehow, as it always seems to, the conversation centered on women, and their place in a man's world. Gus said a woman's place is in the home, so I promptly shot him through the head. Genghis said he thought a woman was a necessary evil. I nudged Sammy and Sammy shot Genghis right through the head. Then I asked Sammy what he thought a woman was, and Sammy without hesitating for an instant shot *me* through the head.

Moral: It's safer to bring a sandwich to the office.

"The Lady and the Cannon"

LAST NIGHT, at a drive-in movie, I was run over on my way to the men's room. Not a very pleasant experience. I tore my pajamas, dropped my pizza, spilled my Pepsi and the baby. I barely made it back to the car in time for the intermission fun. (Don't tell me *you* don't shine your spotlight on the screen, during intermission!) But, in spite of everything, it was a very worthwhile evening. I go along with Louella, *The Lady and the Cannon* is a very good terrific movie. And the cast is very good and terrific too. Clarissa Von Vroom, who looks exactly like Ava Gardner, plays the heroine who falls in love with this cannon, because it reminds her of a Daisy air rifle she had when she was a girl back on the old plantation in Beverly Hills. And the male star is that exciting new find, whose picture was on the cover of *Life* magazine not long ago. His name is Sonny Schnecken, and he looks a lot like Ava Gardner, too. Of course, Sir Lawrence Gleckle is in the picture. *He* doesn't look like Ava Gardner. In fact, he doesn't even *try* to. You know how he *underplays* everything.

The picture has a very unusual opening. It looks like a western, because the first thing you see is this wagon train slowly crossing the plains, with of course, Frankie Laine singing in the background. The scenery is *beautiful*. In fact, it's so beautiful, it gives you a false sense of security, which is exactly what the producer had planned on, because suddenly from literally nowhere comes ten thousand blood-thirsty Apache Indians, a-rippin', a-rappin', and a-rapin'! The camera *zooms* in for some real nice close shots of this, and it's great in color. Then suddenly, and again from nowhere, come the credits—crawling all over the picture, and by the time the credits are finished, you've forgotten what picture you were watching. But it really doesn't matter, because you never see the Indians or the covered wagons again.

Now the screen starts to widen. It gets wider and wider and wider, and just when you think it can't possibly get any wider, you hear a loud "Boinnng!" and the whole thing snaps back to its original size. (If this all seems confusing, forget it. Turn to another chapter.)

Now the picture you came to see starts. It all happens a hundred years ago in Spain and it opens on a shot of this cannon. Actually, the largest cannon in the world (in those days), it's about fifty feet long and with wheels at least ten feet high, and round. And this huge cannon is being dragged along by Clarissa Von Vroom, Sonny Schnecken, and Sir Lawrence Gleckle. This ensures the picture's success. Remember Bogie dragging that boat through the African swamp? Then there was Jimmy Cagney dragging that girl by the hair. That's why they're dragging this big cannon around the country. There's an old maxim among picture-makers: "If you want to be a success in Hollywood, drag something."

Actually the reason Clarissa and Sonny and Sir Lawrence are dragging this cannon around is because they want to take a shot at somebody on the other side of the mountain, for some high and mighty purpose like striking a blow for freedom or something, but it turns out later, they're just a bunch of bandits and they're on their way to stick up a castle.

But the picture isn't all blood and thunder and swashbuckling. There *is* a love story connected with it. Sonny is in love with Clarissa, who doesn't *know* this, because Clarissa is in love with Sir Lawrence, who in turn is unaware of Clarissa's great passion for him, because he's had his monocle painted over to keep out strangers and is quite out of touch with the world in general, and Clarissa in particular.

Poor Sonny slowly reaches the point where his frustration turns his mind and one evening around the campfire he gets fresh with Clarissa, who being the fiery Gypsy that she is, slaps him across the face with an Argyle sock filled with broken glass.

Attracted by the gay sound of tinkling, Sir Lawrence asks what's going on? When Sonny tells him that Clarissa has just slapped him across the puss with an Argyle sockful of broken glass, Sir Lawrence laughs (actually it's about the only laugh in the whole picture). This makes Sonny sore and the next day he refuses to pull *his* share of the cannon. But the imperturbable Sir Lawrence is imperturbed by this, because he knows he can straighten Sonny out in a hurry, by slapping him across the puss with an Argyle sockful of broken glass. It's about here that Sessue Hayakawa sidles up to Sonny and says something about saving face, which is Sessue's only line in the picture, but he does it very well, and it will, I imagine, help sell this picture in the Japanese market.

The repeated puss slapping creates an air of tension among these former fast friends, and as the days pass and they drag the cannon wearily up hill and down dale, across rivers and through deserts, the air becomes almost electric with their pent-up hatred of each other. But finally they arrive at their destination, the castle they have sworn to attack and conquer. Almost at once, Clarissa, Sonny, and Sir Lawrence forget their own animosities and concentrate on their long-sought common goal. Carefully they check the cannon. Then after quick calculation they aim it—directly at the heart of the ancient castle. Then Sonny turns to Sir Lawrence, "Okay—hand me a cannon ball."

"Waddya mean," says Sir Lawrence. "I thought *you* had 'em!"

Then they both turn slowly to Clarissa and she says, "Don't look at *me!*"

Personally, *I* thought it was a very *abrupt* ending for a movie.

42

**THIS IS YOUR SUBMARINE
KEEP IT TIDY!**

KICK THE HAPPINESS HABIT— BECOME A WRITER

HERE'S what T. B. of Tucson, Arizona has to say about the Krine Institute: "All my life I dreamed about being a writer and now, thanks to the Krine Institute of Successful Literary Effort, I am. Just like Professor Krine taught me for three hundred and twenty-three dollars, every day I said to myself two hundred thousand times: 'I am a writer! I am a writer! I am a writer!' Then for an extra three hundred and twenty-three dollars, Professor Krine was kind enough to send me a recording that said 'I am a writer! I am a writer! I am a writer!' two hundred thousand times *for* me, which gave me time for other things like sleeping. Of course, once Professor Krine made a slight mistake and sent me the wrong recording, which turned out to be a parakeet training record and all I can say is *you* listen to 'I am a pretty bird' two hundred thousand times in one day! It's enough to make you fly around the room. And we did. Gladys, my wife, broke her arm. She lost altitude a little too fast."

* * *

Would you like to be a successful writer like T. B. of Tucson, Arizona? Would you be willing to spend a few hours a week learning to write so you may earn an extra fifteen or twenty dollars a year? Or maybe as high as forty, or fifty, or maybe even sixty, on a full-time basis? Never have opportunities for a writer been greater than they are right now, what with minstrel shows, Chautauquas, and vaudeville going full blast. And you don't have to be a "genius" to succeed. Many successful writers are *not* geniuses (no matter what they tell you). Many Krine Institute beginners earn while learning.

Since beginning the course (in 1802), the sales of William J. Werblin of Stoned, Mississippi, have totaled $2,687 (not bad for an illiterate plow horse). F. E. Froonby of Loose, Texas, sold his first story for $16.00; James J. Link is selling half-hour TV scripts for $30.00, fifteen-minute scripts for $15.00, and one-minute scripts for 75¢. (Many sponsors have been buying thirty one-minute scripts from Mr. Link; they figure they come out better in the end.) Kelvin Truncate of West Palm Beach, Wyoming, has made over three hundred sales since he finished the Krine Institute course, five years ago. (The Hong Kong Fortune Cooky Company has bought almost everything he has ever written—a splendid record indeed!)

*   *   *

DON'T WAIT ANY LONGER! Why shouldn't you be a successful writer and live in Beverly Hills and have a swimming pool and a barbecue pit and a funny barbecue apron? Just X the coupon below and we'll send you our De Luxe writing kit and unwanted hair remover (an extra we hadn't mentioned till now). Remember the *Maine,* the *Alamo,* and *Moss Hart!*

THE KRINE INSTITUTE OF SUCCESSFUL LITERARY EFFORT

**Box 802 Little Diomede Island S.W.
c/o Bering Straight.**

Please send me the stuff you talked about new writers getting started and all. I have enclosed my bank book and insurance policies.

Mr.
Miss ....
Mrs.
Madam

Address: ....

44

BOSTON IS A GYPSY

A new musical by Tennessee Gleckle

Starring

CHET HUNTLEY & MOLLY BEE

also starring

RIP TORN—GOUGED GAHAGAN, & DRAWN QUARTERED

and introducing Broadway's newest ingenue,

MISS BITCH BENSON.

This is a science-fiction-horror musical comedy story, as seen through the eyes of a boy and his dog.

The music is by

Rodgers and Hammerstein and Rin-Tin-Tin.

With additional lyrics by

Sax Rohmer, Erle Stanley Gardner, Doctor Spock, and The Thing.

SYNOPSIS OF SCENES

ACT I.

Scene 1: A penthouse cellar.

Scene 2: A first-class stateroom on the S.S. Titanic.

Scene 3: A first-class lifeboat.

Scene 4: The steam room at Vic Tanny's.

Scene 5: Vic Tanny.

Scene 6: Forest Lawn.

ACT II.

Scene 1: A bedroom on the way to Levittown.

Scene 2: A bedroom at Buckingham Palace.

Scene 3: A bedroom on West 49th Street.

Scene 4: A corner drugstore.

Scene 5: Lobby of the Nile-Hilton Hotel.

Scene 6: A Red Sea opening.

Scene 7: A first-class lifeboat.

MUSICAL NUMBERS

ACT I.

Doctor Schweitzer Needs the Serum More Than I Need You..................Clara Barton & the Girls.

I Could Have Cuttysarked All Night...Biff & the Boys.

I'd Rather Be a Bengal Lancer Than Sikh! Sikh! Sikh!
Ralf and Shirley.

Somewhere in This Dirty Old World There Must Be a Dirty Old Man for a Dirty Old Lady Like Me
Louie & Keely

Who'll Squeeze Your Sterno When I'm Far Away
Chiquita Wino and The Girls.

ACT II.

We're Raisin in the Sun What We Should Be Raisin' Under the Moon .....Mary Pickford, Blanche Sweet, Nita Naldi, & the Boys.

You're Number One in My Number Two Book
Ukulele Ike & Tobey Wing.

Have Hump—Will Travel ....Erwin Rommel & the Girls of the Camel Corps.

Tannhäuser ....Buddy Rogers & Mary Brian.

The Wedding of the Painted Doll and the Fire Island Bartender ....Chang & Eng.

Finale ......The entire company—Plus Artie Shaw and His All-Wife Orchestra.

UNDERSTUDIES FOR "BOSTON IS A GYPSY"

Clara Barton—Yvonne De Carlo Chiquita Wino—Grappa Gounod Biff—Boff Buddy Rogers—Mary Brian Mary Brian—Buddy Rogers Buddy Brian—Mary Rogers Tobey Wing—Mrs. Roosevelt Ukulele Ike—Van Cliburn Erwin Rommel—Jacques Tati

Note: Costumes in nudist colony scene by Cole of California *(Skin dept.).*

Note: The title *Boston Is a Gypsy* is based on four words found in Webster's *New World Dictionary.*

T. G.

45

Miami Beach

or

*"Hey You with the
Webbed Feet! Outa the
Pool!"*

THE LAST TIME I visited Miami Beach, Florida, among the many fascinating souvenirs I purchased was a young Seminole Indian girl, whom I brought back to New York with me to do my laundry, just in case someone should ask: *"Who* does your laundry—a *Seminole Indian girl?"* I simply nod my head and say, "Yes." (Sometimes it takes hours and hours to work the conversation around to *"Who* does your laundry—a *Seminole Indian girl?"* but I feel it's worth it.)

Of course, sometimes, *nobody* ever says, *"Who* does your laundry—a *Seminole Indian girl?"* These people are dealt with summarily. They are simply asked to step out on the terrace to enjoy the *view,* and the next thing they know they are *part* of it. Cruel? Yes.

There's a place in Miami Beach, where you can buy a little *live* alligator, which makes an ideal gift, wrapped in a plain wrapper, to send to a dear friend with a heart condition, a large insurance policy, and a beautiful wife. Cruel? Yes.

Who does *your* laundry?

There's also a place in Miami Beach that will sell you a pair of live alligators (full grown male and female) so you may, if you so wish—grow your own brief case. (And just the gift for a Madison Avenue advertising man who likes to live dangerously, even *after* he has left the office for the day.)

Right in back of the Roney-Gleckle, which is near the Eden-Gleckle on South Collins Avenue, there's a cosy little bar, called Boozeland (it's right next to Booze City) where they have, I think, the most exotic drinks, outside of the islands (Riker's and Welfare). For example, they have an extremely alliterative drink there called the "Kentucky Kolonel Kocktail," a very simple concoction, one part gin and one part Dixie Cup. (Incidentally, I understand that the Dixie people are working on a paper cup that's been impregnated with alcohol, so in the future there won't be any waste.) Progress, eh, Herbie?

Boozeland also will shoot your cocktail directly into your veins, if you so desire. This is so the noisy tinkling of the ice doesn't break the spell.

And Boozeland doesn't forget the kiddies, either, which is a good idea—after all, *they're* gonna grow up someday. A potential customer earned is a potential customer made, that's what Maxie the bartender always says. That's why he's dreamed up this special cocktail for the kiddies. It's the Kiddie Martini, one part Pablum, one part strained carrots, and two parts vodka. (Incidentally, this is a very good drink for the *old folks,* too.) Just one or two of these Kiddie Martinis and Grandma and Grandpa will spend many happy hours in the wading pool (trying to get out). Give 'em something to do, eh, Herbie?

A lot of people who have seen the guy wrestle with the alligators, as part of a side trip around the Everglades, have scoffed at what they consider merely a theatrical turn, albeit in the middle of a swamp, but anyway, theatrical. They think the *alligators* are *doped* —they're *not.* The *guy* is.

Miami Beach is where I met the lovely Telefunken Twins. I could *never* tell them apart. So I never tried. Cruel? Yes.

Who does *your* laundry? A *Seminole Indian girl?* Herbie, you're *mad!*

Bellevue

BELLEVUE is a wonderful New York hospital, where people are usually taken for observation, after they've been under observation *before* they're taken for observation. It is known as The Chock Full of Nuts Hotel. In other words—it's a country club for the wet-sheet set, where they have no furniture, just the rooms are upholstered.

New York has many interesting places like Bellevue —for instance, there's Bedloe's Island, where the Statue of Liberty is located. Mr. Bedloe still lives there, and he's still a little surprised—when they asked his permission to erect a statue on his front lawn he didn't

114

expect anything like *that!* But he says it *does* keep the crab grass down.

Another very interesting place in New York is Grant's Tomb. There's a wonderful view from Grant's Tomb—it overlooks the Hudson River. That was Mrs. Grant's idea—a tomb with a view. They *were* thinking about putting in a picture window.

Another very interesting thing to do if you're visiting New York is to take a trip around Manhattan Island on a skin-diver. (Better wear slacks.)

Then visit Tin Pan Alley, where all the hit songs are written. You can even see the piano where Irving Berlin didn't write all those wonderful songs. (They're all written by Cole Porter's butler, who has access to Cole Porter's wastebasket.)

CHAPTER
47

MY DEAR GLADYS:

For your information "An Evening with Jerome Kern, at the Pierre Hotel" does *not* mean in his *room!* Goodbye!

Clyde

"This is the best new work of fiction I have read in years...a book that demands comparison with the very best books of our century...." —GERALD SYKES in *The New York Times*

Lawrence Durrell's JUSTINE

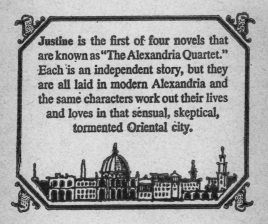

Justine is the first of four novels that are known as "The Alexandria Quartet." Each is an independent story, but they are all laid in modern Alexandria and the same characters work out their lives and loves in that sensual, skeptical, tormented Oriental city.

Want to know
THE REAL JACK PAAR?

- ▶ You watch him on TV!
- ▶ Everyone writes about him!
- ▶ Now read about the most controversial man in show-business today—oops, tonight.
- ▶ Laugh through the hilarious autobiography by the man who changed the sleeping habits of a nation.

Here's how TV's favorite conversation piece views his viewers:

"HE:

33.4 years old, married 2.1 times, lives with 3.2 other people, wears ½ of his pajamas (the bottoms)...

"SHE:

29.2 years old, measures 28-35-40, went to 7.2 schools, wears ½ of a pair of pajamas (the tops)..."

Here's how he looks at himself:

"...just like any other fellow with a wife and daughter, a pleasant house in the suburbs, a Mercedes convertible, twenty-seven pairs of imported sun glasses and an hour and three-quarters TV show..."

I KID YOU NOT (available in a GIANT CARDINAL edition, GC 103) is frank, terse, fraught with the left-field humor and controversy that makes Jack Paar an institution.

Yours for only 50¢